# The Epistle of Polycarp to the Philippians

# The Epistle of Polycarp to the Philippians

## Polycarp

# The Epistle of Polycarp to the Philippians

© Lighthouse Publishing 2019

Written by: Polycarp (A.D. 69 – 155)
Edited by: Alexander Roberts, D.D. (May 12th, 1826 – March 8th, 1901)
Edited by: James Donaldson, LL.D. (April 26th, 1831 – March 1915)
Updated into Modern U.S English: A.M. Overett (b. 1960)

All rights reserved. Without limiting the rights under copyright reserved above, no part of this publication may be reproduced, stored in a retrieval system, or transmitted, in any form or by any means (electronic, mechanical, photocopying, recording or otherwise), without the prior written permission of the copyright owner of this book.

Published by
Lighthouse Publishing
SAN 257-4330
5531 Dufferin Drive
Savage, Minnesota, 55378
United States of America

www.lighthouseebooks.com

Introductory Note to the Epistle of Polycarp to the Philippians

[a.d.65–100–155.] TheEpistle of Polycarp is usually made a sort of preface to those of Ignatius, for reasons which will be obvious to the reader. Yet he was born later, and lived to a much later period. They seem to have been friends from the days of their common pupilage under St. John; and there is nothing improbable in the conjecture of Usher, that he was the "angel of the church in Smyrna," to whom the Master says, "Be thou faithful unto death, and I will give thee a crown of life." His pupil Irenæus gives us one of the very few portraits of an apostolic man which are to be found in antiquity, in a few sentences which are a picture: "I could describe the very place in which the blessed Polycarp sat and taught; his going out and coming in; the whole tenor of his life; his personal appearance; how he would speak of the conversations he had held with John and with others who had seen the Lord. How did he make mention of their words and of whatever he had heard from them respecting the Lord." Thus he unconsciously tantalizes our reverent curiosity. Alas! that such conversations were not written for our learning. But there is a wise Providence in what is withheld, as well as in the inestimable treasures we have received.

Irenæus will tell us more concerning him, his visit to Rome, his rebuke of Marcion, and incidental anecdotes, all which are instructive. The expression which he applied to Marcion is found in this Epistle. Other facts of interest are found in the Martyrdom, which follows in these pages. His death, in extreme old age under the first of the Antonines, has been variously dated; but we may accept the date we have given, as rendered probable by that of the Paschal question, which he so lovingly settled with Anicetus, Bishop of Rome.

The Epistle to the Philippians is the more interesting as denoting the state of that beloved church, the firstborn of European churches, and so greatly endeared to St. Paul. It abounds in practical wisdom, and is rich in Scripture and Scriptural allusions. It reflects the spirit of St. John, alike in its lamb-like and its aquiline features: he is as loving as the beloved disciple himself when he speaks of Christ and his church, but "the son of thunder" is echoed in his rebukes of threatened corruptions in faith and morals. Nothing can be more clear than his view of the doctrines of grace; but he writes like the disciple of St. John, though in perfect harmony with St. Paul's hymn-like eulogy of Christian love.

The following is the original Introductory Notice:—

The authenticity of the following Epistle can on no fair grounds be questioned. It is abundantly established by external testimony, and is also supported by the internal evidence. Irenæus says (Adv. Hær., iii. 3): "There is extant an Epistle of Polycarp written to the Philippians, most satisfactory, from which those that have a mind to do so may learn the character of his faith," etc. This passage is embodied by Eusebius in his Ecclesiastical History(iv. 14); and in another place the same writer refers to the Epistle before us as an undoubted production of Polycarp (Hist. Eccl., iii. 36). Other ancient testimonies might easily be added, but are superfluous, inasmuch as there is a general consent among scholars at the present day that we have in this letter an authentic production of the renowned Bishop of Smyrna.

Of Polycarp's life little is known, but that little is

highly interesting. Irenæus was his disciple, and tells us that "Polycarp was instructed by the apostles, and was brought into contact with many who had seen Christ" (Adv. Hær., iii. 3; Euseb. Hist. Eccl., iv. 14). There is also a very graphic account given of Polycarp by Irenæus in his Epistle to Florinus, to which the reader is referred. It has been preserved by Eusebius (Hist. Eccl., v. 20).

The Epistle before us is not perfect in any of the Greek mss.which contain it. But the chapters wanting in Greek are contained in an ancient Latin version. While there is no ground for supposing, as some have done, that the whole Epistle is spurious, there seems considerable force in the arguments by which many others have sought to prove chap. xiii. to be an interpolation.

The date of the Epistle cannot be satisfactorily determined. It depends on the conclusion we reach as to some points, very difficult and obscure, connected with that account of the martyrdom of Polycarp which has come down to us. We shall not, however, probably be far wrong if we fix it about the middle of the second century.

## The Epistle of Polycarp to the Philippians

Polycarp, and the presbyters with him, to the Church of God sojourning at Philippi: Mercy to you, and peace from God Almighty, and from the Lord Jesus Christ, our Saviour, be multiplied.

### Chapter I.—Praise of the Philippians.

I have greatly rejoiced with you in our Lord Jesus Christ, because ye have followed the example of true love [as displayed by God], and have accompanied, as became you, those who were bound in chains, the fitting ornaments of saints, and which are indeed the diadems of the true elect of God and our Lord; and because the strong root of your faith, spoken of in days long gone by, endureth even until now, and bringeth forth fruit to our Lord Jesus Christ, who for our sins suffered even unto death, [but] "whom God raised from the dead, having loosed the bands of the grave." "In whom, though now ye see Him not, ye believe, and believing, rejoice with joy unspeakable and full of glory;" into which joy many desire to enter, knowing that "by grace ye are saved, not of works," but by the will of God through Jesus Christ.

### Chapter II.—An exhortation to virtue.

"Wherefore, girding up your loins," "serve the Lord in fear" and truth, as those who have forsaken the vain, empty talk and error of the multitude, and "believed in Him who raised up our Lord Jesus Christ from the dead, and gave Him glory," and a throne at His right hand. To Him all things in heaven and on earth are subject. Him every spirit serves. He comes as the Judge of the living and the dead. His blood will God require of those who do not believe in Him. But He who raised Him up from the dead will raise up us also, if we do His will, and walk in His commandments, and love what He loved, keeping ourselves from all unrighteousness, covetousness, love of money, evil-speaking, false witness; "not rendering evil for evil, or railing for railing," or blow for blow, or cursing for cursing, but being mindful of what the Lord said in His teaching: "Judge not, that ye be not judged; forgive, and it shall be forgiven unto you; be merciful, that ye may obtain mercy; with what measure ye mete, it shall be measured to you again;" and once more, "Blessed are the poor, and those that are persecuted for righteousness' sake, for theirs is the kingdom of God."

Chapter III.—Expressions of personal unworthiness.

These things, brethren, I write to you concerning righteousness, not because I take anything upon myself, but because ye have invited me to do so. For neither I, nor any other such one, can come up to the wisdom of the blessed and glorified Paul. He, when among you, accurately and stedfastly taught the word of truth in the presence of those who were then alive. And when absent from you, he wrote you a letter, which, if you carefully study, you will find to be the means of building you up in that faith which has been given you, and which, being followed by hope, and preceded by love towards God, and Christ, and our neighbour, "is the mother of us all." For if any one be inwardly possessed of these graces, he hath fulfilled the command of righteousness, since he that hath love is far from all sin.

Chapter IV.—Various exhortations.

"But the love of money is the root of all evils." Knowing, therefore, that "as we brought nothing into the world, so we can carry nothing out," let us arm ourselves with the armour of righteousness; and let us teach, first of all, ourselves to walk in the commandments of the Lord. Next, [teach] your wives [to walk] in the faith given to them, and in love and purity tenderly loving their own husbands in all truth, and loving all [others] equally in all chastity; and to train up their children in the knowledge and fear of God. Teach the widows to be discreet as respects the faith of the Lord, praying continually for all, being far from all slandering, evil-speaking, false-witnessing, love of money, and every kind of evil; knowing that they are the altar of God, that He clearly perceives all things, and that nothing is hid from Him, neither reasonings, nor reflections, nor any one of the secret things of the heart.

Chapter V.—The duties of deacons, youths, and virgins.

Knowing, then, that "God is not mocked," we ought to walk worthy of His commandment and glory. In like manner should the deacons be blameless before the face of His righteousness, as being the servants of God and Christ, and not of men. They must not be slanderers, double-tongued, or lovers of money, but temperate in all things, compassionate, industrious, walking according to the truth of the Lord, who was the servant of all. If we please Him in this present world, we shall receive also the future world, according as He has promised to us that He will raise us again from the dead, and that if we live worthily of Him, "we shall also reign together with Him," provided only we believe. In like manner, let the young men also be blameless in all things, being especially careful to preserve purity, and keeping themselves in, as with a bridle, from every kind of evil. For it is well that they should be cut off from the lusts that are in the world, since "every lust warreth against the spirit;" and "neither fornicators, nor effeminate, nor abusers of themselves with mankind, shall inherit the kingdom of God," nor those who do things inconsistent and unbecoming. Wherefore, it is needful to abstain from all these things, being subject to the presbyters and deacons, as unto God and Christ. The virgins also must walk in a blameless and pure conscience.

Chapter VI.—The duties of presbyters and others.

And let the presbyters be compassionate and merciful to all, bringing back those that wander, visiting all the sick, and not neglecting the widow, the orphan, or the poor, but always "providing for that which is becoming in the sight of God and man;" abstaining from all wrath, respect of persons, and unjust judgment; keeping far off from all covetousness, not quickly crediting [an evil report] against any one, not severe in judgment, as knowing that we are all under a debt of sin. If then we entreat the Lord to forgive us, we ought also ourselves to forgive; for we are before the eyes of our Lord and God, and "we must all appear at the judgment-seat of Christ, and must every one give an account of himself." Let us then serve Him in fear, and with all reverence, even as He Himself has commanded us, and as the apostles who preached the Gospel unto us, and the prophets who proclaimed beforehand the coming of the Lord [have alike taught us]. Let us be zealous in the pursuit of that which is good, keeping ourselves from causes of offence, from false brethren, and from those who in hypocrisy bear the name of the Lord, and draw away vain men into error.

Chapter VII.—Avoid the Docetæ, and persevere in fasting and prayer.

"For whosoever does not confess that Jesus Christ has come in the flesh, is antichrist;" and whosoever does not confess the testimony of the cross, is of the devil; and whosoever perverts the oracles of the Lord to his own lusts, and says that there is neither a resurrection nor a judgment, he is the first-born of Satan. Wherefore, forsaking the vanity of many, and their false doctrines, let us return to the word which has been handed down to us from the beginning; "watching unto prayer," and persevering in fasting; beseeching in our supplications the all-seeing God "not to lead us into temptation," as the Lord has said: "The spirit truly is willing, but the flesh is weak."

Chapter VIII.—Persevere in hope and patience.

Let us then continually persevere in our hope, and the earnest of our righteousness, which is Jesus Christ, "who bore our sins in His own body on the tree," "who did no sin, neither was guile found in His mouth," but endured all things for us, that we might live in Him. Let us then be imitators of His patience; and if we suffer for His name's sake, let us glorify Him. For He has set us this example in Himself, and we have believed that such is the case.

Chapter IX.—Patience inculcated.

I exhort you all, therefore, to yield obedience to the word of righteousness, and to exercise all patience, such as ye have seen [set] before your eyes, not only in the case of the blessed Ignatius, and Zosimus, and Rufus, but also in others among yourselves, and in Paul himself, and the rest of the apostles. [This do] in the assurance that all these have not run in vain, but in faith and righteousness, and that they are [now] in their due place in the presence of the Lord, with whom also they suffered. For they loved not this present world, but Him who died for us, and for our sakes was raised again by God from the dead.

Chapter X.—Exhortation to the practice of virtue.

Stand fast, therefore, in these things, and follow the example of the Lord, being firm and unchangeable in the faith, loving the brotherhood, and being attached to one another, joined together in the truth, exhibiting the meekness of the Lord in your intercourse with one another, and despising no one. When you can do good, defer it not, because "alms delivers from death." Be all of you subject one to another "having your conduct blameless among the Gentiles," that ye may both receive praise for your good works, and the Lord may not be blasphemed through you. But woe to him by whom the name of the Lord is blasphemed! Teach, therefore, sobriety to all, and manifest it also in your own conduct.

Chapter XI.—Expression of grief on account of Valens.

I am greatly grieved for Valens, who was once a presbyter among you, because he so little understands the place that was given him [in the Church]. I exhort you, therefore, that ye abstain from covetousness, and that ye be chaste and truthful. "Abstain from every form of evil." For if a man cannot govern himself in such matters, how shall he enjoin them on others? If a man does not keep himself from covetousness, he shall be defiled by idolatry, and shall be judged as one of the heathen. But who of us are ignorant of the judgment of the Lord? "Do we not know that the saints shall judge the world?" as Paul teaches. But I have neither seen nor heard of any such thing among you, in the midst of whom the blessed Paul laboured, and who are commended in the beginning of his Epistle. For he boasts of you in all those Churches which alone then knew the Lord; but we [of Smyrna] had not yet known Him. I am deeply grieved, therefore, brethren, for him (Valens) and his wife; to whom may the Lord grant true repentance! And be ye then moderate in regard to this matter, and "do not count such as enemies," but call them back as suffering and straying members, that ye may save your whole body. For by so acting ye shall edify yourselves.

Chapter XII.—Exhortation to various graces.

For I trust that ye are well versed in the Sacred Scriptures, and that nothing is hid from you; but to me this privilege is not yet granted. It is declared then in these Scriptures, "Be ye angry, and sin not," and, "Let not the sun go down upon your wrath." Happy is he who remembers this, which I believe to be the case with you. But may the God and Father of our Lord Jesus Christ, and Jesus Christ Himself, who is the Son of God, and our everlasting High Priest, build you up in faith and truth, and in all meekness, gentleness, patience, longsuffering, forbearance, and purity; and may He bestow on you a lot and portion among His saints, and on us with you, and on all that are under heaven, who shall believe in our Lord Jesus Christ, and in His Father, who "raised Him from the dead." Pray for all the saints. Pray also for kings, and potentates, and princes, and for those that persecute and hate you, and for the enemies of the cross, that your fruit may be manifest to all, and that ye may be perfect in Him.

Chapter XIII.—Concerning the transmission of epistles.

Both you and Ignatius wrote to me, that if any one went [from this] into Syria, he should carry your letter with him; which request I will attend to if I find a fitting opportunity, either personally, or through some other acting for me, that your desire may be fulfilled. The Epistles of Ignatius written by him to us, and all the rest [of his Epistles] which we have by us, we have sent to you, as you requested. They are subjoined to this Epistle, and by them ye may be greatly profited; for they treat of faith and patience, and all things that tend to edification in our Lord. Any more certain information you may have obtained respecting both Ignatius himself, and those that were with him, have the goodness to make known to us.

## Chapter XIV.—Conclusion.

These things I have written to you by Crescens, whom up to the present time I have recommended unto you, and do now recommend. For he has acted blamelessly among us, and I believe also among you. Moreover, ye will hold his sister in esteem when she comes to you. Be ye safe in the Lord Jesus Christ. Grace be with you all. Amen.

## Introductory Note to the Epistle Concerning the Martyrdom of Polycarp

Internalevidence goes far to establish the credit which Eusebius lends to this specimen of the martyrologies, certainly not the earliest if we accept that of Ignatius as genuine. As an encyclical of one of "the seven churches" to another of the same Seven, and as bearing witness to their aggregation with others into the unity of "the Holy and Catholic Church," it is a very interesting witness, not only to an article of the creed, but to the original meaning and acceptation of the same. More than this, it is evidence of the strength of Christ perfected in human weakness; and thus it affords us an assurance of grace equal to our day in every time of need. When I see in it, however, an example of what a noble army of martyrs, women and children included, suffered in those days "for the testimony of Jesus," and in order to hand down the knowledge of the Gospel to these boastful ages of our own, I confess myself edified by what I read, chiefly because I am humbled and abashed in comparing what a Christian used to be, with what a Christian is, in our times, even at his best estate.

That this Epistle has been interpolated can hardly be doubted, when we compare it with the unvarnished specimen, in Eusebius. As for the "fragrant smell" that came from the fire, many kinds of wood emit the like in burning; and, apart from Oriental warmth of colouring, there seems nothing incredible in the narrative if we except "the dove" (chap. xvi.), which, however, is probably a corrupt reading, as suggested by our translators. The blade was thrust into the martyr's left side; and this, opening the heart, caused the outpouring of a flood, and not a mere trickling. But, though Greek thus amended is a plausible conjecture, there seems to have been nothing of the kind in the copy quoted by Eusebius. On the other hand, note the truly catholic and scriptural testimony: "We love the martyrs, but the Son of God we worship: it is impossible for us to worship any other."

Bishop Jacobson assigns more than fifty pages to this martyrology, with a Latin version and abundant notes. To these I must refer the student, who may wish to see this attractive history in all the light of critical scholarship and, often, of admirable comment.

The following is the original Introductory Notice:—

The following letter purports to have been written by the Church at Smyrna to the Church at Philomelium, and through that Church to the whole Christian world, in order to give a succinct account of the circumstances attending the martyrdom of Polycarp. It is the earliest of all the Martyria, and has generally been accounted both the most interesting and authentic. Not a few, however, deem it interpolated in several passages, and some refer it to a much later date than the middle of the second century, to which it has been commonly ascribed. We cannot tell how much it may owe to the writers (chap. xxii.) who successively transcribed it. Great part of it has been engrossed by Eusebius in his Ecclesiastical History (iv. 15); and it is instructive to observe, that some of the most startling miraculous phenomena recorded in the text as it now stands, have no place in the narrative as given by that early historian of the Church. Much discussion has arisen respecting several particulars contained in this Martyrium; but into these disputes we do not enter, having it for our aim simply to present the reader with as faithful a translation as possible of this very interesting monument of Christian antiquity.

The Encyclical Epistle of the Church at Smyrna Concerning the Martyrdom of the Holy Polycarp

The Church of God which sojourns at Smyrna, to the Church of God sojourning in Philomelium, and to all the congregations of the Holy and Catholic Church in every place: Mercy, peace, and love from God the Father, and our Lord Jesus Christ, be multiplied.

Chapter I.—Subject of which we write.

We have written to you, brethren, as to what relates to the martyrs, and especially to the blessed Polycarp, who put an end to the persecution, having, as it were, set a seal upon it by his martyrdom. For almost all the events that happened previously [to this one], took place that the Lord might show us from above a martyrdom becoming the Gospel. For he waited to be delivered up, even as the

Lord had done, that we also might become his followers, while we look not merely at what concerns ourselves but have regard also to our neighbours. For it is the part of a true and well-founded love, not only to wish one's self to be saved, but also all the brethren.

Chapter II.—The wonderful constancy of the martyrs.

All the martyrdoms, then, were blessed and noble which took place according to the will of God. For it becomes us who profess86greater piety than others, to ascribe the authority over all things to God. And truly, who can fail to admire their nobleness of mind, and their patience, with that love towards their Lord which they displayed?—who, when they were so torn with scourges, that the frame of their bodies, even to the very inward veins and arteries, was laid open, still patiently endured, while even those that stood by pitied and bewailed them. But they reached such a pitch of magnanimity, that not one of them let a sigh or a groan escape them; thus proving to us all that those holy martyrs of Christ, at the very time when they suffered such torments, were absent from the body, or rather, that the Lord then stood by them, and communed with them. And, looking to the grace of Christ, they despised all the torments of this world, redeeming themselves from eternal punishment by [the suffering of] a single hour. For this reason the fire of their savage executioners appeared cool to them. For they kept before their view escape from that fire which is eternal and never shall be quenched, and looked forward with the eyes of their heart to those good things which are laid up for such as endure; things "which ear hath not heard, nor eye seen, neither have entered into the heart of man," but were revealed by the Lord to them, inasmuch as they were no longer men, but had already become angels. And, in like manner, those who were condemned to the wild beasts endured dreadful tortures, being stretched out upon beds full of spikes, and subjected to various other kinds of torments, in order that, if it were possible, the tyrant might, by their lingering tortures, lead them to a denial [of Christ].

Chapter III.—The constancy of Germanicus. The death of Polycarp is demanded.

For the devil did indeed invent many things against them; but thanks be to God, he could not prevail over all. For the most noble Germanicus strengthened the timidity of others by his own patience, and fought heroically with the wild beasts. For, when the proconsul sought to persuade him, and urged him90to take pity upon his age, he attracted the wild beast towards himself, and provoked it, being desirous to escape all the more quickly from an unrighteous and impious world. But upon this the whole multitude, marvelling at the nobility of mind displayed by the devout and godly race of Christians, cried out, "Away with the Atheists; let Polycarp be sought out!"

Chapter IV.—Quintus the apostate.

Now one named Quintus, a Phrygian, who was but lately come from Phrygia, when he saw the wild beasts, became afraid. This was the man who forced himself and some others to come forward voluntarily [for trial]. Him the proconsul, after many entreaties, persuaded to swear and to offer sacrifice. Wherefore, brethren, we do not commend those who give themselves up [to suffering], seeing the Gospel does not teach so to do.

Chapter V.—The departure and vision of Polycarp.

But the most admirable Polycarp, when he first heard [that he was sought for], was in no measure disturbed, but resolved to continue in the city. However, in deference to the wish of many, he was persuaded to leave it. He departed, therefore, to a country house not far distant from the city. There he stayed with a few [friends], engaged in nothing else night and day than praying for all men, and for the Churches throughout the world, according to his usual custom. And while he was praying, a vision presented itself to him three days before he was taken; and, behold, the pillow under his head seemed to him on fire. Upon this, turning to those that were with him, he said to them prophetically, "I must be burnt alive."

Chapter VI.—Polycarp is betrayed by a servant.

And when those who sought for him were at hand, he departed to another dwelling, whither his pursuers immediately came after him. And when they found him not, they seized upon two youths [that were there], one of whom, being subjected to torture, confessed. It was thus impossible that he should continue hid, since those that betrayed him were of his own household. The Irenarch then (whose office is the same as that of the Cleronomus), by name Herod, hastened to bring him into the stadium. [This all happened] that he might fulfil his special lot, being made a partaker of Christ, and that they who betrayed him might undergo the punishment of Judas himself.

Chapter VII.—Polycarp is found by his pursuers.

His pursuers then, along with horsemen, and taking the youth with them, went forth at supper-time on the day of the preparation with their usual weapons, as if going out against a robber. And being come about evening [to the place where he was], they found him lying down in the upper room of a certain little house, from which he might have escaped into another place; but he refused, saying, "The will of God be done." So when he heard that they were come, he went down and spake with them. And as those that were present marvelled at his age and constancy, some of them said. "Was so much effort made to capture such a venerable man?" Immediately then, in that very hour, he ordered that something to eat and drink should be set before them, as much indeed as they cared for, while he besought them to allow him an hour to pray without disturbance. And on their giving him leave, he stood and prayed, being full of the grace of God, so that he could not cease for two full hours, to the astonishment of them that heard him, insomuch that many began to repent that they had come forth against so godly and venerable an old man.

Chapter VIII.—Polycarp is brought into the city.

Now, as soon as he had ceased praying, having made mention of all that had at any time come in contact with him, both small and great, illustrious and obscure, as well as the whole Catholic Church throughout the world, the time of his departure having arrived, they set him upon an ass, and conducted him into the city, the day being that of the great Sabbath. And the Irenarch Herod, accompanied by his father Nicetes (both riding in a chariot), met him, and taking him up into the chariot, they seated themselves beside him, and endeavoured to persuade him, saying, "What harm is there in saying, Lord Cæsar, and in sacrificing, with the other ceremonies observed on such occasions, and so make sure of safety?" But he at first gave them no answer; and when they continued to urge him, he said, "I shall not do as you advise me." So they, having no hope of persuading him, began to speak bitter words unto him, and cast him with violence out of the chariot, insomuch that, in getting down from the carriage, he dislocated his leg [by the fall]. But without being disturbed, and as if suffering nothing, he went eagerly forward with all haste, and was conducted to the stadium, where the tumult was so great, that there was no possibility of being heard.

Chapter IX.—Polycarp refuses to revile Christ.

Now, as Polycarp was entering into the stadium, there came to him a voice from heaven, saying, "Be strong, and show thyself a man, O Polycarp!" No one saw who it was that spoke to him; but those of our brethren who were present heard the voice. And as he was brought forward, the tumult became great when they heard that Polycarp was taken. And when he came near, the proconsul asked him whether he was Polycarp. On his confessing that he was, [the proconsul] sought to persuade him to deny [Christ], saying, "Have respect to thy old age," and other similar things, according to their custom, [such as],

"Swear by the fortune of Cæsar; repent, and say, Away with the Atheists." But Polycarp, gazing with a stern countenance on all the multitude of the wicked heathen then in the stadium, and waving his hand towards them, while with groans he looked up to heaven, said, "Away with the Atheists." Then, the proconsul urging him, and saying, "Swear, and I will set thee at liberty, reproach Christ;" Polycarp declared, "Eighty and six years have I served Him, and He never did me any injury: how then can I blaspheme my King and my Saviour?"

Chapter X.—Polycarp confesses himself a Christian.

And when the proconsul yet again pressed him, and said, "Swear by the fortune of Cæsar," he answered, "Since thou art vainly urgent that, as thou sayest, I should swear by the fortune of Cæsar, and pretendest not to know who and what I am, hear me declare with boldness, I am a Christian. And if you wish to learn what the doctrines of Christianity are, appoint me a day, and thou shalt hear them." The proconsul replied, "Persuade the people." But Polycarp said, "To thee I have thought it right to offer an account [of my faith]; for we are taught to give all due honour (which entails no injury upon ourselves) to the powers and authorities which are ordained of God. But as for these, I do not deem them worthy of receiving any account from me."

Chapter XI.—No threats have any effect on Polycarp.

The proconsul then said to him, "I have wild beasts at hand; to these will I cast thee, except thou repent." But he answered, "Call them then, for we are not accustomed to repent of what is good in order to adopt that which is evil; and it is well for me to be changed from what is evil to what is righteous." But again the proconsul said to him, "I will cause thee to be consumed by fire, seeing thou despisest the wild beasts, if thou wilt not repent." But Polycarp said, "Thou threatenest me with fire which burneth for an hour, and after a little is extinguished, but art ignorant of the fire of the coming judgment and of eternal punishment, reserved for the ungodly. But why tarriest thou? Bring forth what thou wilt."

Chapter XII.—Polycarp is sentenced to be burned.

While he spoke these and many other like things, he was filled with confidence and joy, and his countenance was full of grace, so that not merely did it not fall as if troubled by the things said to him, but, on the contrary, the proconsul was astonished, and sent his herald to proclaim in the midst of the stadium thrice, "Polycarp has confessed that he is a Christian." This proclamation having been made by the herald, the whole multitude both of the heathen and Jews, who dwelt at Smyrna, cried out with uncontrollable fury, and in a loud voice, "This is the teacher of Asia, the father of the Christians, and the overthrower of our gods, he who has been teaching many not to sacrifice, or to worship the gods." Speaking thus, they cried out, and besought Philip the Asiarch to let loose a lion upon Polycarp. But Philip answered that it was not lawful for him to do so, seeing the shows of wild beasts were already finished. Then it seemed good to them to cry out with one consent, that Polycarp should be burnt alive. For thus it behooved the vision which was revealed to him in regard to his pillow to be fulfilled, when, seeing it on fire as he was praying, he turned about and said prophetically to the faithful that were with him, "I must be burnt alive."

Chapter XIII.—The funeral pile is erected.

This, then, was carried into effect with greater speed than it was spoken, the multitudes immediately gathering together wood and fagots out of the shops and baths; the Jews especially, according to custom, eagerly assisting them in it. And when the funeral pile was ready, Polycarp, laying aside all his garments, and loosing his girdle, sought also to take off his sandals,—a thing he was not accustomed to do, inasmuch as every one of the faithful was always eager who should first touch his skin. For, on account of his holy life, he was, even before his martyrdom, adorned with every kind of good. Immediately then they surrounded him with those substances which had been prepared for the funeral pile. But when they were about also to fix him with nails, he said, "Leave me as I am; for He that giveth me strength to endure the fire, will also enable me, without your securing me by nails, to remain without moving in the pile."

Chapter XIV.—The prayer of Polycarp.

They did not nail him then, but simply bound him. And he, placing his hands behind him, and being bound like a distinguished ram [taken] out of a great flock for sacrifice, and prepared to be an acceptable burnt-offering unto God, looked up to heaven, and said, "O Lord God Almighty, the Father of thy beloved and blessed Son Jesus Christ, by whom we have received the knowledge of Thee, the God of angels and powers, and of every creature, and of the whole race of the righteous who live before thee, I give Thee thanks that Thou hast counted me worthy of this day and this hour, that I should have a part in the number of Thy martyrs, in the cup of thy Christ, to the resurrection of eternal life, both of soul and body, through the incorruption [imparted] by the Holy Ghost. Among whom may I be accepted this day before Thee as a fat and acceptable sacrifice, according as Thou, the ever-truthful God, hast foreordained, hast revealed beforehand to me, and now hast fulfilled. Wherefore also I praise Thee for all things, I bless Thee, I glorify Thee, along with the everlasting and heavenly Jesus Christ, Thy beloved Son, with whom, to Thee, and the Holy Ghost, be glory both now and to all coming ages. Amen."

Chapter XV.—Polycarp is not injured by the fire.

When he had pronounced this amen, and so finished his prayer, those who were appointed for the purpose kindled the fire. And as the flame blazed forth in great fury, we, to whom it was given to witness it, beheld a great miracle, and have been preserved that we might report to others what then took place. For the fire, shaping itself into the form of an arch, like the sail of a ship when filled with the wind, encompassed as by a circle the body of the martyr. And he appeared within not like flesh which is burnt, but as bread that is baked, or as gold and silver glowing in a furnace. Moreover, we perceived such a sweet odour [coming from the pile], as if frankincense or some such precious spices had been smoking there.

Chapter XVI.—Polycarp is pierced by a dagger.

At length, when those wicked men perceived that his body could not be consumed by the fire, they commanded an executioner to go near and pierce him through with a dagger. And on his doing this, there came forth a dove, and a great quantity of blood, so that the fire was extinguished; and all the people wondered that there should be such a difference between the unbelievers and the elect, of whom this most admirable Polycarp was one, having in our own times been an apostolic and prophetic teacher, and bishop of the Catholic Church which is in Smyrna. For every word that went out of his mouth either has been or shall yet be accomplished.

Chapter XVII.—The Christians are refused Polycarp's body.

But when the adversary of the race of the righteous, the envious, malicious, and wicked one, perceived the impressive nature of his martyrdom, and [considered] the blameless life he had led from the beginning, and how he was now crowned with the wreath of immortality, having beyond dispute received his reward, he did his utmost that not the least memorial of him should be taken away by us, although many desired to do this, and to become possessors of his holy flesh. For this end he suggested it to Nicetes, the father of Herod and brother of Alce, to go and entreat the governor not to give up his body to be buried, "lest," said he, "forsaking Him that was crucified, they begin to worship this one." This he said at the suggestion and urgent persuasion of the Jews, who also watched us, as we sought to take him out of the fire, being ignorant of this, that it is neither possible for us ever to forsake Christ, who suffered for the salvation of such as shall be saved throughout the whole world (the blameless one for sinners), nor to worship any other. For Him indeed, as being the Son of God, we adore; but the martyrs, as disciples and followers of the Lord, we worthily love on account of their extraordinary affection towards their own King and Master, of whom may we also be made companions and fellow-disciples!

Chapter XVIII.—The body of Polycarp is burned.

The centurion then, seeing the strife excited by the Jews, placed the body in the midst of the fire, and consumed it. Accordingly, we afterwards took up his bones, as being more precious than the most exquisite jewels, and more purified than gold, and deposited them in a fitting place, whither, being gathered together, as opportunity is allowed us, with joy and rejoicing, the Lord shall grant us to celebrate the anniversary of his martyrdom, both in memory of those who have already finished their course, and for the exercising and preparation of those yet to walk in their steps.

Chapter XIX.—Praise of the martyr Polycarp.

This, then, is the account of the blessed Polycarp, who, being the twelfth that was martyred in Smyrna (reckoning those also of Philadelphia), yet occupies a place of his own in the memory of all men, insomuch that he is everywhere spoken of by the heathen themselves. He was not merely an illustrious teacher, but also a pre-eminent martyr, whose martyrdom all desire to imitate, as having been altogether consistent with the Gospel of Christ. For, having through patience overcome the unjust governor, and thus acquired the crown of immortality, he now, with the apostles and all the righteous [in heaven], rejoicingly glorifies God, even the Father, and blesses our Lord Jesus Christ, the Saviour of our souls, the Governor of our bodies, and the Shepherd of the Catholic Church throughout the world.

Chapter XX.—This epistle is to be transmitted to the brethren.

Since, then, ye requested that we would at large make you acquainted with what really took place, we have for the present sent you this summary account through our brother Marcus. When, therefore, ye have yourselves read this Epistle, be pleased to send it to the brethren at a greater distance, that they also may glorify the Lord, who makes such choice of His own servants. To Him who is able to bring us all by His grace and goodness into his everlasting kingdom, through His only-begotten Son Jesus Christ, to Him be glory, and honour, and power, and majesty, for ever. Amen. Salute all the saints. They that are with us salute you, and Evarestus, who wrote this Epistle, with all his house.

Chapter XXI.—The date of the martyrdom.

Now, the blessed Polycarp suffered martyrdom on the second day of the month Xanthicus just begun, the seventh day before the Kalends of May, on the great Sabbath, at the eighth hour. He was taken by Herod, Philip the Trallian being high priest, Statius Quadratus being proconsul, but Jesus Christ being King for ever, to whom be glory, honour, majesty, and an everlasting throne, from generation to generation. Amen.

Chapter XXII.—Salutation.

We wish you, brethren, all happiness, while you walk according to the doctrine of the Gospel of Jesus Christ; with whom be glory to God the Father and the Holy Spirit, for the salvation of His holy elect, after whose example the blessed Polycarp suffered, following in whose steps may we too be found in the kingdom of Jesus Christ!

These things Caius transcribed from the copy of Irenæus (who was a disciple of Polycarp), having himself been intimate with Irenæus. And I Socrates transcribed them at Corinth from the copy of Caius. Grace be with you all.

And I again, Pionius, wrote them from the previously written copy, having carefully searched into them, and the blessed Polycarp having manifested them to me through a revelation, even as I shall show in what follows. I have collected these things, when they had almost faded away through the lapse of time, that the Lord Jesus Christ may also gather me along with His elect into His heavenly kingdom, to whom, with the Father and the Holy Spirit, be glory for ever and ever. Amen.

ompliance